to the people of Katoomba and Leura

past and present

KATOOMBA & LEURA Illustrated

Robert & Evelyne Ralston

First published in 2013 by Writelight Pty Ltd
for Robert and Evelyne Ralston
Email: robertralston22@yahoo.com

ISBN 978-0-9874340-8-1

Produced by Victoria Jefferys www.writelight.com.au
Pre-press by Graphic Print Group, Adelaide
Printed in China by 1010 Printing International Ltd

the beginning was in the Dreamtime...

Three Sisters
- a tragic love story.

In the dreamtime, the ancestral spirits of the Australian Aborigines wandered the earth and created everything in it.

The most popular Gundungurra dreaming of the creation of the Three Sisters at Katoomba is a tragic love story.

Three beautiful Gundungurra sisters fell in love with three brothers who were warriors of the Dahrug, but marriage between these two peoples was forbidden by tribal law.

When the brothers arrived with a warring party to claim the sisters, the Kuradjuri (clever man) of the Gundungurra used his magic powers to turn the sisters into stone. He hoped that this would protect the sisters until the brothers had left.

In the fighting that followed, the Kuradjuri was unfortunately killed....

... and the three sisters can still be seen to this day, frozen in stone .... perhaps forever.

The First People

The Blue Mountains is Aboriginal land. It was occupied by two major tribal groups: the Gundungurra of the Jamison and Megalong Valleys, and the Dahrug of the Cumberland Plains.

The Gundungurra and Dahrug peoples lived in the higher mountains during the warmer seasons. Their rock carvings, spear grooves, rock shelters and tools and other artifacts have been dated back over 22,000 years.

Much of the ancient evidence was found in 'the Gully' area, in the heart of Katoomba itself.

The indigenous people of Australia walked softly.
They lived in a natural harmony with the land, its wildlife and vegetation, and its cycles and seasons. The signs of their impact are very subtle and can be difficult to find.

The Gully

William Lynch
(Mawiack)

"The Gully" was a summer camping place that was well known to travelling Aborigines since prehistoric times. Its spring is a source of the Katoomba Falls.

The first great waves of migration to Australia came with the discovery of its gold. Katoomba is on the main route to the goldfields of Ophir and Sofala, and to Hill End where the world's largest single piece of gold (the Holtermann Nugget) was found.

Many indigenous Australians constructed permanent homes in the Gully (Garguree) following the Gold Rushes, when the swelling numbers of European and Chinese immigrants had made their traditional and mobile lifestyle impossible.

Jimmy Shepherd and Frank Cooper in the Gully

The Gully was a refuge for the poor. It became emblematic of Aboriginal dispossession when all of its residents were evicted in the late 1950s after their continuous occupation for over 60 years, to make way for the construction of the Catalina Park motor-racing circuit.

The circuit was closed after only 18 years of operation.

The Gully was formally recognised as an Aboriginal Place in 2002.

It is now the site of an 'interpretive walk' which is constructed to illustrate and acknowledge its long and indigenous heritage.

Catalina Park

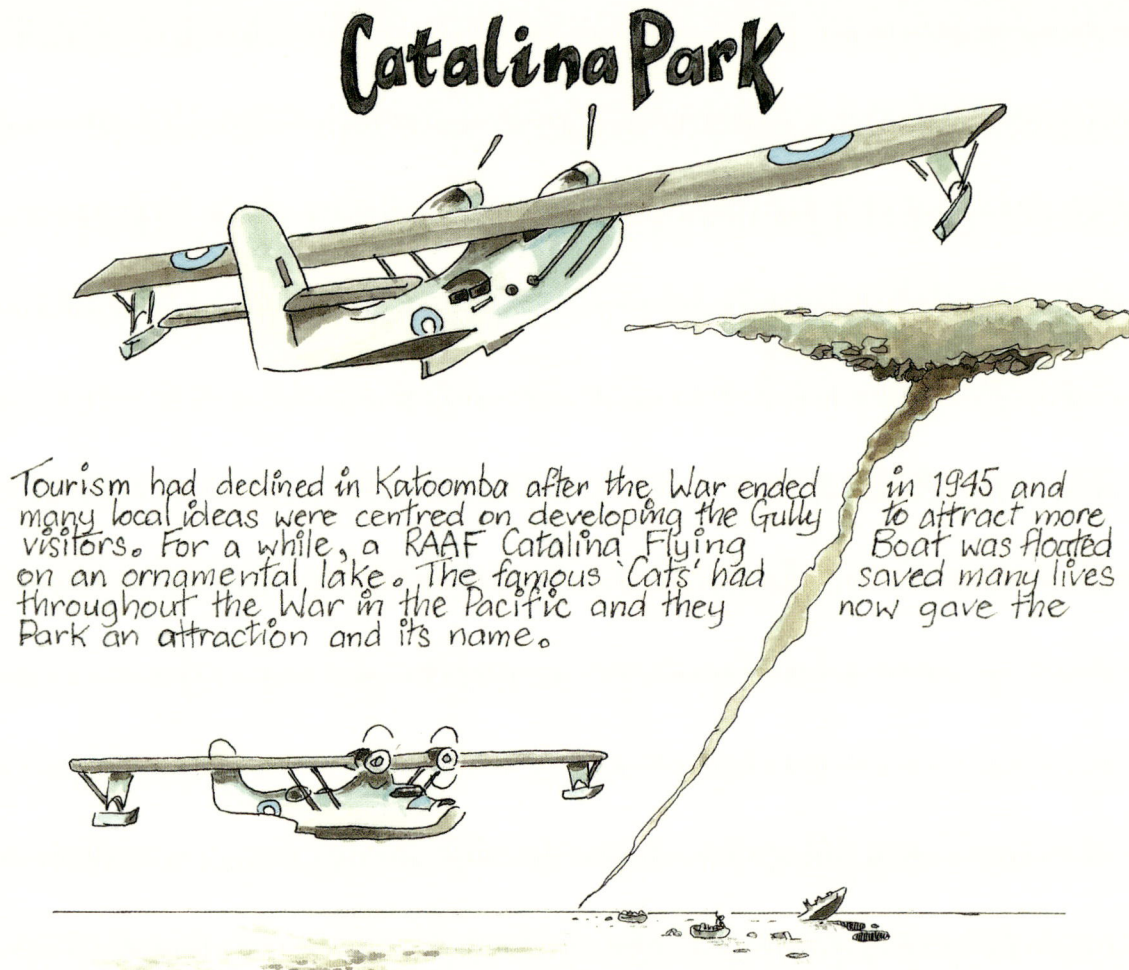

Tourism had declined in Katoomba after the War ended in 1945 and many local ideas were centred on developing the Gully to attract more visitors. For a while, a RAAF Catalina Flying Boat was floated on an ornamental lake. The famous `Cats' had saved many lives throughout the War in the Pacific and they now gave the Park an attraction and its name.

The motor-racing circuit was proposed in 1949, but it wasn't completed until 1961. It held many successful race meetings. It had frequent accidents and two reported deaths. The vagaries of mountain weather was a major cause of the circuit's early closure in 1979. The circuit is still intact and is now accessible to walkers and cyclists.

The circuit is 2.1Km long. It has 3 'hairpin' turns and is tightly contained within steel and hardwood barriers. The mountain climate made it often foggy, wet and slippery. Nevertheless, it was a fast circuit but it had no escape roads or 'soft crash' areas.

Start/Finish
Lake
The tunnel
Aquatic Centre

Its dangers are known to the authors of this book as Robert raced here in the mid-1960s.

Robert on a 250cc Ducati.

He has vivid memories of how close the fence was at the apex of 'the tunnel'; the name given to the circuit's final corner.

The Aviators

Australians love aviation. This feeling may rise from the vast distances of a land that is over 30 times larger than Britain but with only 1/3rd of its population.

Katoomba has shown this affection by its parks.

Catalina Park is named after an aircraft.

Kingsford Smith Park is named after the first pilot to fly across the Pacific, from the USA to Australia, in 1928.

Bert Hinkler Park was named after Bert made the first solo flight from Britain to Australia.

Smithy

Melrose Park is named after a pilot whose exploits included being the only solo to finish in the ill-fated Melbourne Centenary Air Race in 1934.

KINGSFORD SMITH
MEMORIAL PARK

Early aviation was risky.
All three flyers died in air
crashes. Only Bert Hinkler
had reached the age of 40.

Bert Hinkler

Charles 'Jimmy' Melrose

Bert Hinkler Park

Why Katoomba chose to name so many of its parks this
way is a mystery. One local suggests that it may have
something to do with 'altitude'.

A mining town

Like many other early settlements in Australia, Katoomba began as a mining town. Coal and shale were mined from 1879. A major difficulty was finding a way to lift the heavy ore nearly 300 metres from the mines to the Great Western Railway siding.

The problem was solved when Norman Selfe designed the steepest railway incline in the world. This has become today's Scenic Railway.

By the time that the mines closed in 1945, Katoomba was already moving on a new path with the development of tourism and the recognition of the beauty of its surroundings.

The relics of a mining past
might still be seen in Katoomba's
Scenic Railway and the occasional
restored miner's cottage....
or in the chance discovery of
an old tunnel, platform, cable or
boiler in the tangle of its forests.

Norman Selfe

about 1885

The Landslide

When a large crack appeared across the top of Dogface Rock in late 1930, mining was thought to be the major cause. For several months, tourists gathered, hoping to be present when the cliff fell. Nothing happened and interest waned.

The first fall came at 4am on Wednesday 28th January 1931 and gave off tremors that were felt 20 Km away in Mount Victoria.

By the end of the year, nearly 100,000 cubic metres had fallen, closing the mines below but with the fortunate result of adding another scenic attraction to the Blue Mountains.

The Landslide is best viewed from here, on the Golden Stairs.

the Golden Stairs

The Salvation Army (known affectionately as the 'Salvos') are woven into a number of Australian myths. These range from the famous SAO biscuits (favoured by Salvation Army Officers) to the naming of the Golden Stairs.

After visiting the miners at the Ruined Castle, the 'Salvos' could be heard singing the Emma Booth-Tucker hymn "Climbing up the golden stairs" as they toiled up the miner's track to Narrow Neck.

O I'm climb-ing up the gold-en stair to Glo - ry, O - I'm climb-ing with my gold-en crown be - fore me

Today, the track is well-used by bushwalkers, and the Salvation Army continues its active presence in Katoomba.

a Scenic World story

This story begins with Harry Hammon. A young man when the Depression began, Harry had a poor education, little money and few prospects. But he was a visionary with grandiose ideas and with no aptitude at all for quitting.

After some success in local transport, Harry, leased the incline railway on its closure in 1945, to develop it as a tourist attraction. There were immense technical problems but Harry persisted and they were overcome.

Skyway - opened in 1958

Many similar projects followed. The materials came from War surplus, closed mines and failed industries. The story of their adaptation reads as a litany of Harry's problem-solving and persistance.

What began as a rail-line and a shed serving hot water and ice cream has evolved to the present complex which provides a range of communal, recreational, artistic and educational activities. 25 million passengers have now ridden on the Scenic Railway.

The Hammon family appear committed to a continued evolution. More seems yet to come.

Katoomba becomes a town

'Katoomba' is a local Aboriginal word that can mean a place of shining, tumbling or falling water. J. B. North registered his mine at Orphan Rock under that name in 1877 and it was soon adopted by the growing settlement which had been known as 'The Crushers'.

The name was given official status when Katoomba became a municipality in 1889.

John Britty North is sometimes referred to as "the father of Katoomba".

Although mining remained the major business of Katoomba, the area was already attracting hunters, fishermen and bushwalkers.

The transition to a tourist centre came in 'fits and starts'. The post-war period until the Great Depression was a boom time.

Katoomba, with its numerous guest houses and its grand hotels, was known as "the honeymoon capital of Australia."

The Carrington

Two impressive grand hotels of the Blue Mountains are the Carrington at Katoomba and the Hydro Majestic at nearby Medlow Bath.

the Hydro Majestic

The Carrington is the highest point of the Katoomba landscape. It is an icon of the town. It took its name from one of its guests: a NSW Governor (1885-1890) Lord Carrington.

Other guests have included the Prince of Wales (1920) - later King Edward VIII and later still to abdicate - and the Duke and Duchess of York (1927).

Lord Carrington

One local myth says that every Prime Minister of Australia has stayed there, until quite recent times.

The chimney is unmistakable. The hotel had its own power station and provided electricity for the whole town until the late 1920's.

The Carrington was the town's last great expression of Victorian architecture, as this gave way to the style that has become more closely identified with Katoomba... Art Deco.

ART DECO

The Art Deco style originated in the Paris Expo of 1925. It was simple yet highly stylistic and it made use of the most modern materials of its time.

Its dominant motifs are bold geometric shapes, symmetry, rich contrasting colours and animal and human forms often inspired by the ancient Mesopotamian and Egyptian cultures. It was widely used in all forms of art and design.

It appealed strongly to Australians and became a major style of the 1920s and 30s. Art Deco objects are readily found in the many 'collectibles' shops of Katoomba. Art Deco style can also be seen in many of its building and older homes, in their designs, stained-glass windows and featured ceilings.

Art Deco is beautifully expressed in the heritage-listed and famous Paragon Cafe in Katoomba Street. It can also be recognised in the facades of Katoomba's old cinemas.

CINEMAS

In 1900, theatres were the centres of entertainment in many Australian towns. Katoomba had two: the Empire and the Kings. They held dances and provided plays, roller-skating and variety shows.

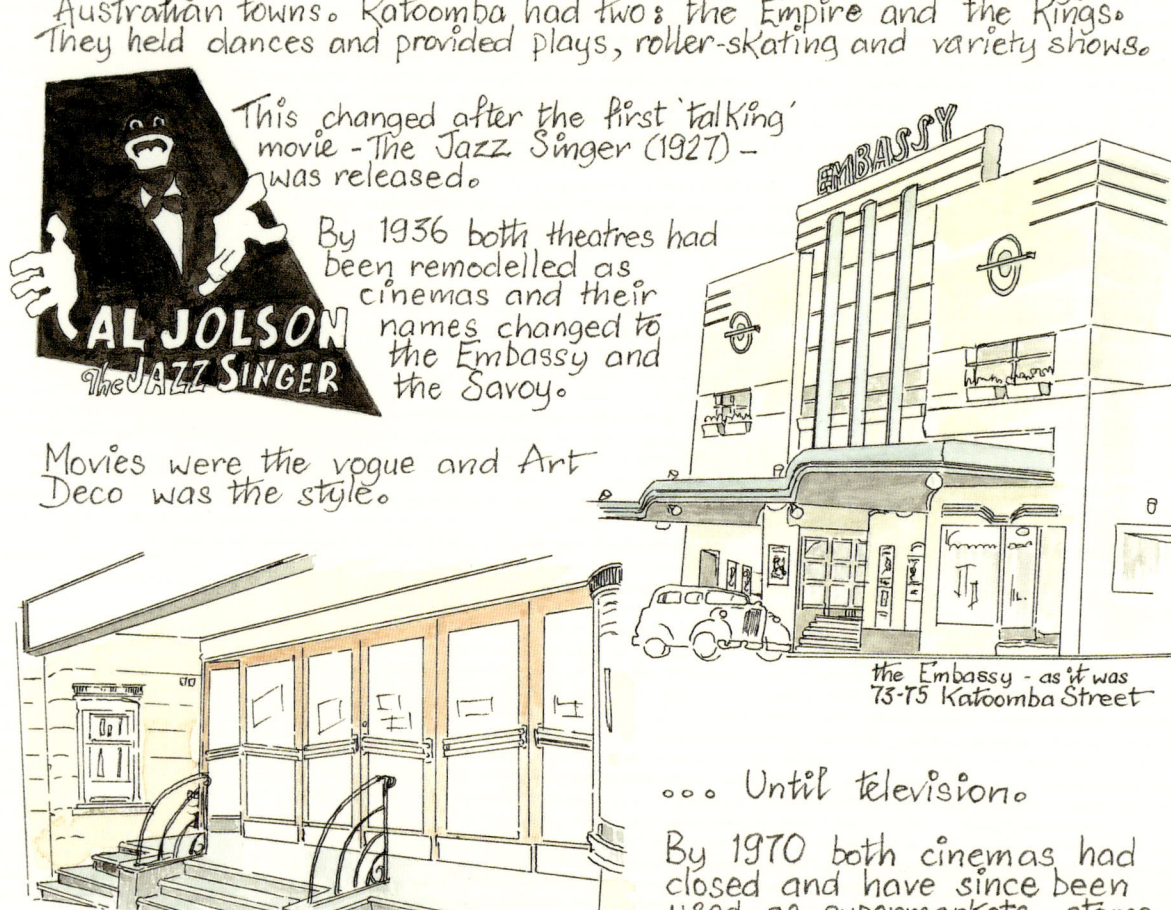

This changed after the first 'talking' movie - The Jazz Singer (1927) - was released.

By 1936 both theatres had been remodelled as cinemas and their names changed to the Embassy and the Savoy.

Movies were the vogue and Art Deco was the style.

the Embassy - as it was
73-75 Katoomba Street

... Until television.

By 1970 both cinemas had closed and have since been used as supermarkets, stores, shops or restaurants.

the Savoy - as it is
18-24 Katoomba Street

By 2000 the theatre had regained its place in the ultra-modern, huge screen, multi-cinema complex of `the edge`.

Until, of course, the next change comes along.

So, when you wander the streets of these old Australian towns and see a building that looks a little bit like a theatre .... it probably was.

a town in a National Park

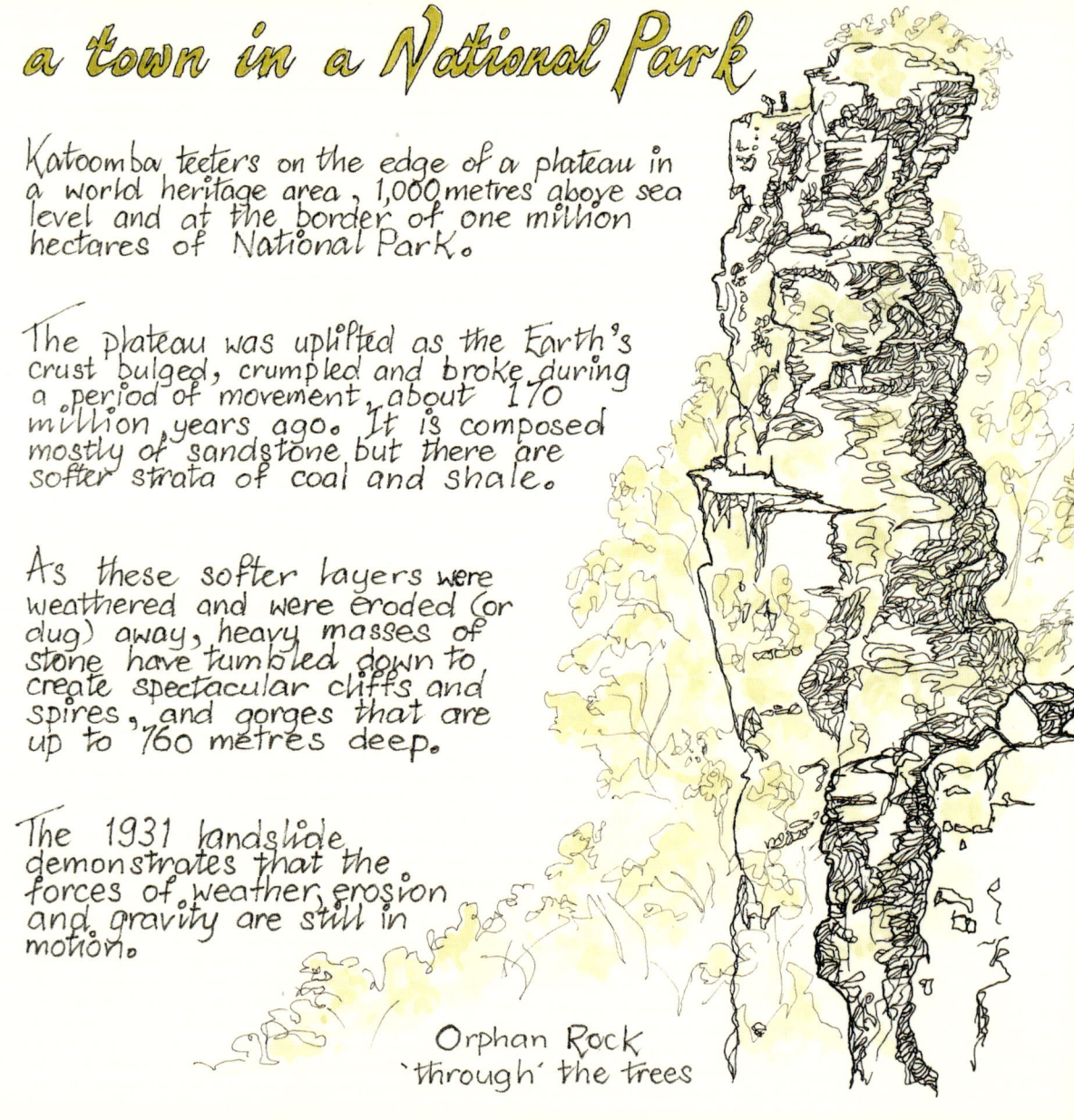

Katoomba teeters on the edge of a plateau in a world heritage area, 1,000 metres above sea level and at the border of one million hectares of National Park.

The plateau was uplifted as the Earth's crust bulged, crumpled and broke during a period of movement, about 170 million years ago. It is composed mostly of sandstone but there are softer strata of coal and shale.

As these softer layers were weathered and were eroded (or dug) away, heavy masses of stone have tumbled down to create spectacular cliffs and spires, and gorges that are up to 760 metres deep.

The 1931 landslide demonstrates that the forces of weather, erosion and gravity are still in motion.

Orphan Rock
'through' the trees

Narrow Neck

This long neck and the plateau that it connects with is 13 kilometres long. It separates the Jamison from the Megalong Valley.

Echo Point
about 1910 —

When it is quiet, face the West and call — and many seconds later an echo will rebound from the faraway Megalong Valley.

Katoomba Falls

A feature of many Blue Mountains waterfalls is their 'double leap'.

Boar's Head

A spectacular and unmistakable rock formation.

The Ruined Castle

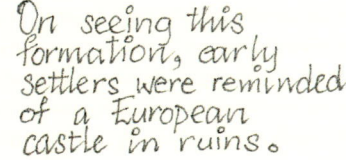

On seeing this formation, early settlers were reminded of a European castle in ruins.

The Witches Leap

There are no prizes for guessing why the Witches Leap was given its name.

Crossing the Blue Mountains

In the first 25 years of British settlement, eight official expeditions were mounted to find a crossing over the Blue Mountains; to be confronted by difficult terrain, waterfalls and a maze of cliffs. All failed.

By 1813 the Australian coastline had been fully mapped for 10 years, but no European had any knowledge of what lay within. The mountains were a 'prison wall'.

In May 1813 three graziers - Blaxland, Lawson and Wentworth - began their successful crossing by following the ridge-line of the present Great Western Highway at Glenbrook. Their progress was slow and incredibly arduous due to the dense brush that existed then, but which has since given way to more open forest.

They left one visible sign of their crossing on a marked tree at Pulpit Hill, near the entry to Katoomba and dangerously close to the highway.

After 18 days and nearly 100 kilometres of unyielding effort, the prison wall was 'broken'.

Pulpit Hill later became the site of local folklore as an unrecorded burial site.
And after two centuries of fires, traffic accidents and other calamities, the marked tree continues to endure.

The Marked Tree

Blaxland

Wentworth

Lawson

The Eucalypts

The marked tree is a eucalyptus.

The eucalyptus is native to Australia. It is also the predominant natural vegetation of the Blue Mountains where it has over 90 different species. They are found in closed forests, in open forests and woodlands, and as stunted mallee shrubs on the plateaus. The most spectacular are the tall Blue Gums, the Blue Mountains Ash, and the Scribbly Gums of the open forest valleys.

Aboriginals use eucalyptus tree leaf infusions in traditional medicines. This was adopted by two surgeons of the First Fleet who distilled the oil from leaves to treat their patients.

The eucalyptus is now cultivated worldwide for its many applications in industry, medicines, pesticides, foodstuffs and fragrances. The Blue Mountains is a living laboratory of eucalyptus. This is one reason for its World Heritage listing.

The Blue Mountains' blue

Any distant object will display some shade of blue due to the phenomenon called 'Rayleigh Scattering'. This is caused by light rays being scattered in many directions by small particles in the air. But the blue haze of the mountains is deeper and different to any found elsewhere in the world.

Eucalyptus trees continually disperse droplets of their oil into the atmosphere. These act as tiny lenses that intensify the scattering of blue light.

The Rainforest

Over 1000 species of plants are found in the Blue Mountains where they have evolved as the result of a particular geology, exposure and climate.

As Australia became drier, the once-great rainforests of the mountains have shrunk to some moist and sheltered areas that can be found among the open forests.

These temperate rainforests are populated by ferns, tree-ferns and moss; and have become the lair of lyre-birds and diamond pythons.

Wollemi Pine

Wollemi pines were previously fossils in museums, amongst other extinct species of the long-vanished Gondwanaland. This 'dinosaur age' pine was thought to have died out nearly two million years ago.

When National Park officer and adventurer, David Noble, discovered 100 living trees in September 1994, his excitement can only be guessed at.

The site of these living fossils — aptly titled 'Wollemia nobilis' — is a closely-guarded secret. But a successful propagation program has now made them available to botanical gardens throughout the world, and to all Australians as our unique Christmas tree.

Flowers

Bottle Brush

Wattle

Spring is the season of flowers. In the Blue Mountains, many of these are peculiar to its altitude and climate.

Flowers can be found in the shrubs and undergrowth of the eucalyptus forests. Others are scattered across the heathlands of the plateaus.

Look closely and you may find grevilleas, banksia, wattle and hakea. You may also find the subtle wax flower, iris and pea flower, but you will not miss the spectacular waratahs and mountain devils.

Banksia

Mountain Devil

The Waratah

Bushfire

Fire has been the dominant evolutionary force in the Australian landscape for the last 50,000 years.

Many native plants need fire for their regeneration; to open their seed pods or to activate their dormant buds.

aftermath Echo Point 2011

While fires start from many natural causes, Aboriginal people used deliberate fires to create a planned mosaic of vegetation at different ages and stages. This 'fire stick farming' maintained an ongoing food supply and made it easier to spot and hunt game.

Importantly, it also protected them from the huge-scale and disastrous fires that have regularly occurred since European settlement. The villages of the Blue Mountains have been saved many times, through the desperate and often-heroic efforts of their firefighters.

Professional firefighters are now adopting Aboriginal methods of controlled burning in cooler months. This reduces the fuel build-up that has been responsible for the worst fires of the last 100 years. It also promotes the regeneration of healthier forests.

our local heroes

The Birds

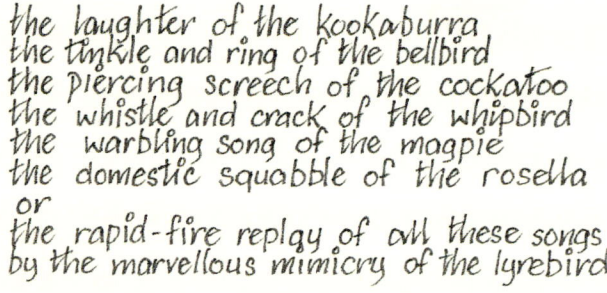

Listen to the birds!

Listen for:
    the laughter of the kookaburra
    the tinkle and ring of the bellbird
    the piercing screech of the cockatoo
    the whistle and crack of the whipbird
    the warbling song of the magpie
    the domestic squabble of the rosella
    or
    the rapid-fire replay of all these songs
    by the marvellous mimicry of the lyrebird.

Kookaburra

Look up for:
    the flight of eagles, hawks and falcons.

Look about for:
    the robins, wrens and honeyeaters.

a White Cockatoo

Robert feeds a friendly King Parrot

Look for the evidence of:

  the currawong who can empty bins in search of food
  the bowerbird who seeks blue objects - flowers, pegs
        and bottletops - to attract a mate
  the lyrebird who turns over the edges of paths, in
        search of insects . . . .

and

Look out for:

  the swooping magpie, who attacks each
  Spring to protect his nest.

There are birds everywhere.

Animals

The Blue Mountains abounds with wildlife.

It's forests and grasslands are home to bats, bandicoots, gliders, wallabies, wombats and kangaroos.

Unlike the birdlife, however, these animals are not easy to see. Many are nocturnal feeders who retreat during the day. Others are timid and are wary of human noises and contact.

The best chance of seeing them comes from moving quietly through their habitats during dusk or early dawn.

Possums and bushrats are exempted.
They can be too often found close to, or inside the houses of Katoomba.

Reptiles

The Katoomba area is home to many reptiles.

Green and brown tree snakes, golden crown snake and red-bellied and eastern brown snakes are commonly found.

The 10 most-venomous snakes in the world are all found in Australia; but they are not necessarily the most dangerous. They are not aggressive and danger can be avoided by walking 'calmly' - if possible - away.

Lizards range from tiny skinks to enormous goannas.

The 'blue-tongue' is an interesting and commonly-found species. It is slow-moving and lacks any real weapons or defence. Its survival relies on a threatening posture while slowly lashing with its spectacular blue tongue. 'Blue' is associated with poison in Nature, and this colour may add to the bluff.

the Creatures

The Bunyip is a fearsome creature who emerges from waterholes and swamps to feast on women and girls.

In one Aboriginal legend, the Three Sisters were turned to stone by their father, who used a magic bone to protect them from a Bunyip.

In the confusion, he dropped the bone and became the lyrebird, scratching and searching for the bone while calling to his daughters.

The Yowie lives in the deep wilderness of the Blue Mountains. Aboriginal legends describe the Yowie as ape-like, hair-covered and hideous. He is the furtive, fast-running "hairy man of the woods."

Yowie sightings occur to the present day. Internet sites and associations are actively collecting the evidence of their footprints, bones, primitive tools, and the occasional photograph.

stay alert!   Be careful!!

Bushwalking

Katoomba was established during the Victorian Age in which strenuous outdoor activity and mountain air were thought to confer many physical and spiritual benefits (a belief still held today).

Local businesses paid for the construction of walks to attract more visitors (eg the Federal Pass in 1900).. and the majority of the tracks that exist today were built between 1880 and the Great War 1914 - 18.

James McKay

The most ambitious was the Giant Stairway proposed by Ranger James McKay. It was started in 1916 but it proved so difficult that it was only completed with cheap Depression-era labour in 1932.

Giant Stairway

The longest is the Six Foot (bridle) Track. Built in 1884, it stretches from the Marked Tree to Jenolan Caves. Later by-passed by motor-roads, it was restored in 1985 for walkers.

For some, walking is not enough. In 1984 the Six Foot Track was first used for a Marathon. With nearly 1,000 entrants, it is now Australia's 5th largest Marathon and its largest off-road running event.

And for others a marathon is not enough. 'Wild Endurance' requires its teams to navigate up to 100 Kms of challenging terrain over 36 hours.

And the 600 'North Face 100' competitors run 100km through the night for up to 27 hours.

And for others, simply reading about these exploits will be enough.

Outdoor Adventure

Intersecting fire trails and paths extend across almost the entire Blue Mountains; and mountain biking is an exciting way to access many spectacular places. The Narrow Neck is one of the best rides in the mountains.

Abseiling began as a climber's way to safely descend but it has become an 'adventure' in its own right. The Boars Head is an exceptional site that provides pitches for the experienced and for the beginner.

'Canyoning' is for the experienced only. As the rope must travel down with the abseilers when they descend multiple pitches, the canyoners must be certain that they can finish what they have started.

And then, of course, there are the climbers.

No mountains can be complete without them.

But not on the Three Sisters. Climbing was banned here in 2000.

But not before many mountaineers had climbed them, including Australia's famous Tim Macartney-Snape.

Rescues

Most of us live in regulated urban environments.
It is not surprising then, that the vastness, mystery, raw
danger and wild beauty of mountain areas can have such
strong appeal to our adventurous spirit.

PLB

PERSONAL LOCATOR BEACON
A PLB can be borrowed at no
cost from Katoomba Police Station.

In the mountains, however, even the
simple adventure of leaving a
path can result in a need for
rescue.

All Blue Mountains rescues are
directed by the NSW Police.
The Police are trained and
well-equipped for the task and
can call on the support of
over 100 State Emergency
Service (SES) volunteers
and on the specialist skills
of the Bushwalkers Wilderness
Rescue Squad.

The Rescuers have a proud record of dedication, sacrifice,
extreme effort and success. But the Police advise that most
rescues could have been avoided, had some reasonable
preparations been undertaken.

The NSW Police and the National Parks Service encourage the use of their 'TREK initiative'

Take supplies of food, water, navigation and First Aid equipment.

Register your route - tell friends and family when you expect to return.

Emergency Beacon - take a PLB.

Keep to your planned route and follow the map and walking trails.

Festivals

There is always something to celebrate in the Blue Mountains. Its villages have a tradition of annual festivals, and many of these take place in Katoomba.

The 'Festival of Walking' celebrates the beauty of nature, and the joy of walking. Not surprisingly, it is held each Spring in October. In January, the Carrington hosts the 'Wines of the West Festival.' This is a showcase of quality wineries and boutique breweries. Together, these festivals provide a sedate and genteel balance to the 'Roaring 20s... and all that Jazz' Festival of February.

This festival is shared with nearby Leura and is high-energy, outrageous and exciting. It captures the post-war euphoria of the 1920s with its saucy clothing and dancing, new social freedom and jazz. Features include a classic 1920's car show, dancing, radio plays, high tea at the Paragon and a grand Art Deco Ball at the Carrington.

The music festival of 'Folk, Blues and Roots' – in March – plays in intimate venues around Katoomba. This is the compelling 'music of the people' and its festival attracts the best of Australian and overseas artists.

But, without a doubt, our favourite is the Winter Magic Festival.

This festival unleashes the extraordinary and unsuspected talents of the community: its costumed acrobats, jugglers, musicians, magicians, dancers, poets, story-tellers, wizards and troubadours.

Each Winter Solstice, Katoomba Street is transformed with market stalls and decorations as the setting for their parade.

Winter Magic Festival

... more Winter Magic

City of the Arts

The Blue Mountains has always attracted artists.

Artists have historically sought out such places that can give them good light, inspirational surroundings, reflective solitude and cheap rent.

Harry Phillips was an early Katoomba photographer whose work still enthralls and inspires artists today. His iconic 'Bridal Veil' is the subject of a mural by Michael Lynn, near the Anglican Church in Katoomba Street.

Katoomba was also the home of Eleanor Dark, author of the historical novel 'A Timeless Land'. Her home, Varuna, now supports a thriving community of writers; as Australia's national residential house for writers.

Varuna - Given to the Eleanor Dark Foundation by her son, Michael Dark, in 1989.

A strong artistic culture is evident in events that sprinkle across the Katoomba calendars in its many private galleries, in 'bentArt' and 'Art Street', in its rich variety of music venues, and in its festivals of writers and of films.

Avian Exuberance
by Terrance Plowright

An innovation is Australia's only rainforest sculpture exhibition, held annually from 2012. The pieces are exhibited along the Scenic World elevated walkway, against the spectacular backdrop of the World Heritage forest.

Aboriginal Art also has a strong presence in Katoomba. A number of organisations are actively promoting indigenous culture through dance, craft, music and art displays.

Art speaks all languages. Australian and overseas visitors are learning to appreciate Aboriginal culture and its understanding and affinity with the land.

Best of all, is the communities support for the Arts; shown by the shopkeepers who display the Art Street works, the many volunteers of the Art Gallery and of the laneway beautification projects (Butterfly Walk), and in the public-funded Arts grants.

Katoomba calls itself a 'City of the Arts'. In 2012 the Council succeeded in a collaboration with Coles Supermarket to give us a Cultural Centre with an Art Gallery that is worthy of the claim.

Lifestyle

Most Australians live near the coast. They enjoy the renowned Australian lifestyle of sunshine, beach and barbeque. But not the few who live on mountain tops and who have made different lifestyle choices.

8000 people live in Katoomba. Like the artists, many are drawn by the beauty of the Blue Mountains. But Katoomba is a long way from the employment centres of the Sydney basin, so the advent of the 1860's rail service established a tradition of the long-distance commuter. Loco driver John Heron took the early morning express for 14 years, so his nickname - 'Big Fish' - was transferred to the train. It seemed only logical that the next, later service was called 'the Chips'. To everyones' delight, the Fish and Chips are still listed as the regular services today.

Katoomba Station

And the same tradition of business commuters goes on; though the i-phone and laptop are gaining ground over the tabloids and cryptic crossword.

Café and food culture is a large part of life in Katoomba. In many respects, Katoomba is blessed by its 1·3 million visitors each year as they support a range of choices not otherwise possible. What other town of 8,000 inhabitants can boast of a Chinese, Malay, Korean, 3 Indian, 4 Thai and 5 Italian restaurants in just over 500 metres of its main street.

Perhaps that is the reason why the street seems to attract the very best of buskers.

Michael

Busker Dave

Katoomba has avoided the invasions and takeover of the major international fast-food franchisers. It does not look like 'every other town'. Indeed, it is one of the first two towns of the Southern Hemisphere to qualify as a member of the Cittaslow 'slow food' association (Goolwa SA is the other); and is also the home of Australia's longest-running Food Cooperative (since 1981).

The modern quality food movement has become inseparable from concerns of bio-diversity, local and organic produce, seasonal diets, fair trading and environmental care.

The Council reflects many of these community concerns and conducts a range of public 'Green' workshops at its recycle centre in North Katoomba.

Evelyne loves to shop at the Co-op.

Lesser known to tourists, North Katoomba offers a sub-urban lifestyle with many hidden treasures. Among these are views over the Grose Valley, Yosemite Park and the spectacular Minnehaha Falls. It also possesses our only community garden.

———✕———

Gardens abound in Katoomba. Like gardens everywhere, they often give insight into the personality and lifestyle of the gardener.

Isabelle's Secret Garden

The weather is cold in Katoomba. People tend to wear more clothes that can sometimes total-up to a distinctive local 'look'. While there are often strong tokens of individuality, the Fashionista can be described as generally sombre in colour with blended elements of recycle, retro, mountaineering and Op shop; and the often crowning influence of one of the biggest hatteries in Australia. Personally, we love it.

A visitor ponders over local styles.

Finally, Katoomba is home to many diverse and 'alternative' lifestyle groups; embracing healing, spirituality, meditation, philosophy and religion. From an 'outsider' perspective, nothing could be said without being trite; except to remark that mountain tops are where people go, to 'seek' or to provide answers.

Leura - the garden village

Katoomba was the focus of early settlement and it had easy access to many outstanding, natural wonders; it was destined to become the administrative and tourist centre of the Blue Mountains.

Nearby Leura is only half the size. Its Western border has merged with Katoomba. It also shares the same origins and history but it would be wrong to think of Leura as an extension or - worse - a 'suburb' of Katoomba. Leura is different.

The difference is obvious on entering the village. Its centre is smaller and is mostly composed of specialised shops and boutiques. It is located on a quaint, narrow and two-level divided street that creates a more intimate atmosphere, and that inhibits the flow and noise of heavy vehicles. It has no back-packer establishments (Katoomba has six) and its guest houses lie outside the centre (unlike Katoomba's). A visit to local agents discloses that real estate prices are much higher in Leura, where there are many historical grand houses and gardens.

Leura is different. Its main street 'mall' has a general absence of buses, bustle and buskers; and a demure and exclusive atmosphere of quiet refinement. This is in contrast to the more noisy, bustling, inclusive and tolerant diversity of Katoomba.

Nevertheless, both places are wedded; in their closeness, their love of the mountains, and in their needs for tourism and for the sharing of facilities that neither place alone could afford.

But they are an odd couple.

Leura Mall

The Mall - at its best
during the Leura Village
Fair in early October when
the cherry trees are in full
blossom.

A heritage village - many
of its buildings were
constructed between
1900 and 1921.

Vignettes de Leura

LONDON PARIS NEW YORK LEURA

LONDON PARIS NEW YORK LEURA

Leura House

Built on the highest
point of Leura in 1880,
Leura House is an
elegant Victorian
guest house on a
grand scale.

It is also a dramatic
survivor of the 1957
fire which destroyed
127 other Leura
properties, including
all those that
surrounded it.

Directly opposite Leura House are the sombre and evocative remains of Chateau Napier; a proud guesthouse of 1910 that perished in the great fire of 2 December 1957.

Leura Cascades
Picnic Area

The Everglades - 1948

The stunning home and gardens designed by Danish architect Paul Sorensen. The gardens remain faithful to the original design and their views have changed little in over 100 years. While open all year, the gardens are a feature of Leura's Spring 'Gardens Festival' when many beautiful private gardens are opened to raise funds for Katoomba Hospital.

Leuralla

Home of the Evatt family that has included a leader of the Federal Labor Party and a President of the United Nations General Assembly. Leuralla is in a Paul Sorensen garden and houses the NSW Toy and Railway Museum. Ginger Meggs is among its collection of iconic toys, books and comics.

The escarpment garden of Leuralla is overlooked by the comic characters Olive Oyl and Boofhead (for those who are old enough to remember). Its early 1900 ampitheatre was restored in 1986 and the Bathurst slate stage has since been the setting for Greek and Shakespearian tragedies, and a music recital by pianist Roger Woodward.

the Ampitheatre

Olive Oyl watches a rehearsal of "Julius Caesar."

Leura Golf Course

We could mention Sublime Point, Leura Cascades, Linda Falls..

... or simply drive around the tree-lined avenues of Leura.

And why not one last stroll —

starting at North Katoomba with a
drink at Gearin's 'pub'.

Art deco, an original
Australian 'long bar,' and
once recently owned by
actor Jack Thompson.

—

The Gearin's

... a wander around the
Peace Memorial and the
1895 Court House ....

...then back across the bridge for a last look around the town...

...or maybe a ride on the Mountains Explorer bus...

... a walk down the main street ...

.. a chance discovery of modern Katoomba ..

... glimpses of Lurline Street ...

... the crowd gathers at Echo Point ...

. a thought for the road builders . . .

at the Road Builders Memorial
- Sculptor - Terrance Plowright

... to finally arrive home.
A good stroll.

The Story of this book
From Paris to Katoomba

Robert was not coping with retirement.

After many years in the military, he was not prepared for his sudden freedom and our days were becoming cycles of planting, pruning, painting and polishing - driven by his endless lists of 'jobs to do.'

He was easily talked into Paris. It is my family home and I spent my first 24 years there. In Paris we would be forced into a French pace and lifestyle and could start our new life from a different perspective. I leased an apartment in the old 'artist quarter' of Montparnasse, on the Left Bank.

Things happened quickly. Robert unexpectedly confessed to a long-suppressed desire to be an artist. We bought sketch pads, joined the library and visited numerous galleries. Soon he was consumed with reading BDs ('bandes dessinees' or French comics) and filling his sketch pads.

One day we spotted a 'Carnet de Paris', an illustrated book on the 15th arrondissement, including the monuments and buildings around Montparnasse. The book was a real treasure and it led us to some excited discussions.

Katoomba could have such a book and it could cover much more than its architecture. We both love Katoomba. I had lived there in the 80s and 90s and had returned, with Robert, seven years ago. It would be a collaborative work: I would do the research; Robert, the illustrations. Before we had left Paris, I was collecting information from the internet, Robert was practising with finer and finer pens.

We had discovered our answer to a 'happy retirement'. On our return to Katoomba, we worked for the next eight months to produce this book. It has been a labour of love!

We hope that you have enjoyed it.

Evelyne & Robert
April 2013

Acknowledgements

The authors and publishers are grateful to the Blue Mountains Library Local Studies for their consent for the use of photographs which provided some models and inspiration for illustrations in this book. While Harry Phillips is the most famed and prominent, there are also many other excellent but unknown photographers to whom this book is indebted.

We also acknowledge the artists who have consented to our illustrations of their works. We are sincerely grateful for the generosity and uplifting support given by Terrance Plowright (Road Builders and Avian Exuberance), Ian Swift (the Bear) and Jason Chatfield (Ginger Meggs).

Our gratitude is also expressed to the musicians Michael and Busker Dave for the inclusion of their images; and to Isabelle Compton for the sneaky peak at her secret garden.

The authors and publishers also acknowledge the courtesy and friendliness of the owners, managers and proprietors who consented to the inclusion of their businesses and undertakings. These include the Paragon, Scenic World, The Carrington, The Edge, Varuna House, The Hatlery, Leuralla, the Mountains Explorer Bus Company, The Lost Bear Gallery, the Food Cooperative, the Salvation Army and the NSW Police Force.

Our final acknowledgements are for the enthusiastic and positive support of our trusted friend and proof-reader Melanie Rivers; and for the encouragement and professional guidance of Victoria Jefferys, to whom we are indebted for more than one good idea that has been included in this book.